SNAKES ARE SCARY

ThaT Say Go Tc ha

Some people love snakes, others fear them. No matter how you feel about snakes, they are an important component of the natural environment.

There are 700 species
of venomous snakes in
the world. Around 250
of those can kill a human
with one bite.

Snake scales are made of keratin, the same material that hair and fingernails are made of.

Snakes lay eggs. Some snakes incubate the eggs in their bodies and give birth to live babies.

When snakes strike
they have a near 100%
success rate.

Some snakes survive
for up to two years
without a meal.

Venomous snakes are poisonous from birth. The young are actually more dangerous than older snakes, because they're more likely to strike. Older snakes usually try to flee.

Snakes can expand the capacity of their jaws due to an elastic jaw ligament.

Snakes have poor eyesight. They use their tongues to detect smells to find food or stay away from enemies.

A snake continues to grow throughout its life. They periodically shed their skin as part of this growing process.

Snakes live on every continent of the world except Antarctica. There are species which swim in the ocean.

Snake charmers in Asia often charm king cobras. The cobra is mesmerized by the shape and movement of the flute, not by the sound.

The Green Anaconda is the heaviest snake in the world. They can weigh as much as 550 lbs and reach an amazing length of 29 feet.

50,000 people a year die from snakebites, but only about 5 die in Australia, where the deadliest snakes live.

Poisonous or venomous snakes inject poison or venom into their prey which starts the digestive process even before the food has been swallowed.